Donn,

I hope these you

touch on your own feelings

of closeness to the earth. . .

David Siegmund

The Meeting Ground

From the Windshadow Press collection

Journeys Into Wild Places

Volume 1

The Meeting Ground

Journeys Into Wild Places

Volume 1

David Siegmund

Windshadow Press

Library of Congress Catalog Card Number: 93-60605
ISBN: 0-9636650-7-3

Publisher's Cataloging Information for Libraries:

Siegmund, David.
The Meeting Ground.
Series: Journeys Into Wild Places.
Volume 1.
1. Natural Areas — Oregon
2. Oregon — Description and Travel 1981-
3. Hiking — Oregon
Classification: 917.95
Library of Congress Catalog Card Number: 93-60605
ISBN: 0-9636650-7-3

First Printing 1993.
Printed in the United States of America.

Windshadow Press
Box 207-A
Westlake, OR 97493

Contents: The Places

For Louis and Dorothy,

and the ones they've given

over to the world.

I have lived a butterfly many times, remembered
as often why I must crawl again. Here, I am close
to the laboring earth. Here, stumbling through
a hundred heavy legs, I learn deeply
the sweetness of flight. Here, descending
to the bondage of a black cocoon, I learn
the delicacy of my wings. Such is the path
to infinite fields of wildflowers.

This time I take as necessity. Patience---that is
the way to my freedom.
Leaf and stem and long days of green:
these are my teachers. Why resist
the balance?

A sea must lap the shore. A seed must
root in darkness to flower in light.
Oak and maple and alder bear a gray nakedness
for their time of brilliance. Rainbows wait for clouds
to collide precisely with sun. The moon wanes
to carry softness into her full light.
Proud rivers rush to oblivion,
to become cloud and rain and dew, to begin again
as infants of obscure hills. Even mountains wear down,
to a vigil for the cataclysm
of rebirth.

Angels, too, surrender wings and remember to crawl,
to rise, and fall, and rise,
to suffer gravity and struggle through a time
of deep weariness, before they pass again
to ethereal flight.

I am not surprised
to awake a caterpillar.

Introduction

Anyone who writes about the natural world can hope to convey only a small piece of its beauty and meaning. It's too wide, too deep, too intricate to be captured whole.

How can we fully speak sunlight after rain, glowing on leaves of vine maple? The majesty of an old spruce bonding earth and sky? The seemingly infinite tones of a creek dropping over ledges and boulders? The vibration of the very earth we stand on, as a winter wave cracks apart on blackrock?

These are things that defy precise communication. No words can ever accurately substitute for being there, face-to-face with this immense life we call "nature." Yet words can point, and whisper occasional truths about the feeling of special places.

The stories in this collection are about walks into wild areas on the Oregon coast, about seeing and hearing through the footsteps.

This book is not a trail guide. It's a blend of images, events, thoughts and feelings, an account of how we perceived the journeys unfolding and related our lives to the wild life that surrounded us.

In all these walks and the wordflows that followed, our abiding rule was: we come as we are. We have no specialized knowledge of the natural world. We're not experts in plants or birds or rocks or coastal ecosystems or the weather fronts that move in around us. The names we use in speaking these journeys only slightly outnumber those we knew as we set out on the trail.

Names aren't the point here. These are stories about perception, about human in the wild. Often we tried to see and hear *without* names, simply feeling into the life of these places. We've not aimed for science. We've aimed for the spirit of the land.

A sense of closeness to that spirit can come from any walk in the wild, and carry over to other contacts with elements of the natural world. When you're out there on your own explorations and begin to feel something magical,---in the sound of a stream, or the light on a leaf, or the wind sweeping across a land you're momentarily part of ---give it your most careful attention. What you're feeling may be very close to the miracle of your own heartbeat.

Close To Home

The day meets us clear and brilliant. Only thin streaks of cloud, stretched from a focus far out to sea, break the pure blue above. Searush fills the air as we begin our ascent to Cook's Ridge on a broad trail through alder forest. New leaves tint the light sliced through the canopy. Our feet sink and slip through mulched remains of last year's crop.

Tall snags poke at the sky from the neighboring slope, skeletons waiting to crumble or crash back to earth. Alders fade away behind us, giving in to a stand of lean fir and hemlock. Our trail and the forest floor to each side become a tangle of branches shed with growth or torn loose by wind. The night's damp air collects on needles and limbs, ticking in droplets against salal and grounded leaves and the growing stillness. Sunlight provokes wet lives into a green glow. Moss and swordfern, huckleberry and the needled fans of lower branches---all seem sharply alert, as though the coastal forest might come even more to life in a collision of water and light.

Old spruce begin to rise around us. Fog stubbornly hangs to the forest, tempering the bright day. The air thickens with water that has little patience for gravity. Armies of molecules climb and swirl on the hint of a breeze, trapping sunlight into hazy white shafts. Space opens among the giant spruce, unwilling to allow here the dense undergrowth of the lower forest.

Mosses and lichens gather freely on whatever surface will have them. Lime green spreads a veneer over rocks and exposed roots and the bases of trees. Shades of olive cling to the high places, wrapping a sheath around limbs, running narrow stripes across trunks, swaying in long strands caught by the whims of an unsteady air. Stalks of jade-green lay a patchwork over the ground, like groves of dwarfed pines that will never exceed their half-inch height. The lichen they call old man's beard scatters in tangled, weightless clumps on twigs and bark, almost an afterthought of the life bent on filling this space.

A wide peace settles on the ridge. The sea has dropped away to a faint rushing. Even the birds have surrendered to quiet. Our eyes float over a field of green and brown, gray and shadow. The day seems to measure itself out in dampness, building slowly, till each drop finds the critical mass and feeds into the rainforest floor.

We slide our fingers over the trunks of a few giants, following wet curls and ripples in bark. Their size and strength feel overpowering. Leaning back, we try to capture the fullness of these ancient lives. But our eyes can never reach to the crown or even the highest limbs from our angle at the base. The young ones nestled in among them also incline toward mystery. Their barks refuse to be identified at our height, all cloaked in the velvet of this wet land. Only a few signs are given---the telltale hemlock branch, heavy with clustered cones; tight-woven needles and prickly skin of fallen spruce branches; the soft, flatter lay of fir needles draped out over the trail.

The path carries us through an erratic course, mapping out its own plan for human eyes. It climbs quickly, drops off and winds upward again, cutting a dark strip from carpets of green and yellow, pinching down to slice between old trunks, drawing our bodies through a stream of patterns and unpredictabilities.

Burnt-orange roots heave through the soil. Black cracks open in the earth for no apparent reason. Giants grown through centuries loom over seedlings with roots from only seasons ago. Ferns push new sprouts up from the heart, letting old fronds droop and die back into the needles. Threads of spider weaving stretch from trunk to trunk, appearing in silver streaks, disappearing against their back-drops, tricking light again and again to flow across a scarcely material path. Golden patches slip through hazy air and the canopy of limbs, to fade and vanish and reawaken on a different ground as fog and earth shift.

Hemlock limbs reach out from the shadows, like broad green wings dreaming flight. Small cones cover a section of trail, not spread here and there randomly over time, but lumped together in a mass of hundreds, as though in a moment of fear for the species, the mother tree cut loose its full litter of possibilities. A middle-aged spruce fallen across the way has been sawed through to allow passage. Rings tell a life of many good years, only a few lean years, as if to say: how well, not how long, is the question of true importance. A single fir needle defies gravity right in front of our faces, floating on air, drifting even higher at a soft touch. Strange, magical, beautifully rebellious at the human mind---but we imagine spider watching, pulling at the lines, toying with the tourists and their inflexible notions of science.

Sounds of the shore have lost us. Stillness seems only to be deepening as we reach the sign to Gwynn Creek and begin our descent. Slowly, the haze among the trees thickens into opaque white. The creek's voice probes up the slope, faint, elusive, struggling against the silent bulk of old trees. Even high above the waterflow, wet air billows up to lay a gloss over the ferns, the slick leaves of salal and huckleberry, the fanned limbs of hemlock and cedar. Blues and greens flash from droplets on the tips of needles. In another step, yellow and red and different drops sparkle with light shot through the web of limbs folded over us.

Sunstreaks gather all around us now, angling through the fog, sorting out their identities by means of shadows cast from high branches. With every few steps, a different constellation of limbs breaks the flow of light, realigning its play against the white drift of molecules. In the nearest beams, we can see the tiny droplets clearly, spinning, falling, surging up on the most delicate impulses of the wind. We reach our senseless fingers in among them, knowing the impossibility of touch, knowing the eyes here to be quicker than the hand. They slip easily past every movement of probing flesh, and resume their freedoms on an unfilled space.

Around a bend, new light punches through the moment's window, pouring streams of heavy rays across the trail. Our eyes fix on visible air, these almost tangible streaks dropped out of the sky. As we approach, a feeling arises of walking fearlessly toward the gate of some deep mystery, as though everything unknown, everything hovering beyond this life, this forest, this world of time and its collage of effects, might somehow be revealed in a swirl of white molecules.

One by one, the veins of light absorb us. Our bodies cut through, from beam to shadow to beam, till air becomes invisible again. We stop and look back, to remember---the gate, the feeling, the will to pierce into the mystery. But the angle of passage has erased the white streams. Only a clear trail lies behind. Fractured light has become whole again, and blended back into the space that carried us

15

farther along.

More beams appear ahead. Most are scattered by the high limbs. But one broad shaft of light stands alone. Driven straight through the canopy and into the forest floor, it feels like a wise, benevolent life, an angel straddling our trail. The presence grows stronger, then fills our vision. We push into it, through it, almost feeling its breath passed over our bodies. But our movement is too intent, too ambitious. A moment of opportunity slides around us. Quickly, we look behind. The angel beam has vanished, back into forest green.

The creek begins to show now, a flickering of whitecaps and gray troughs racing down an alder-thickened corridor. Switchbacks wind us out above water, then back into shallow ravines. Feeding streams cut across our path at nearly every hollow, all drawn from hidden sources on the slope, this mountain of earth and forest so full it has to break seams to spill out. Some trickle faintly, or slip without a sound---almost invisibly---over gleaming blackrock. A few speak boldly enough that we guess they have their own names, dropping through short falls or gurgling over stairstepped rocks.

Each stream, and the channel it carved in more ferocious times, seems a story in itself. Waterflows tear precious soil away from thick roots, till winter storms topple the weakened giants. Old survivors lean away from the hillside, coaxing the young to grab hold and push

for the light, to gamble their lives on ancient wisdom till they're able to sink a grip into black soil. Saplings grope through and around whatever lies near, sprawling out roots like the tentacles of a hungry beast that claims the hollows where other creatures fear to go.

Cones bind on brown needles with hairlike first roots, smelling for earth below. Seeds carried on the wind slide behind the curls of peeling bark, sprouting shrubs and seedlings high above the ground. Spores tuck between flakes of rotting wood; colonies of swordferns burst up, sprinkle out fresh seed, and melt back into their mother logs. Stumps and fallen trunks and disordered limbs coat themselves with bright green, evolving into life-covered sculptures, poised to feed from any angle of the sun. Mosses and delicate maidenhair spread a blanket over the earth, anchoring the slope against itself, saving nutrients for the young yet to come. So many here speak in their own ways of the interpenetration, where birth and seeking, strength and aging, death and decay, weave their faces together.

The cover of undergrowth on the slope beside us thickens. A cool breeze floats down from the ridge. Tall, crooked branches of vine maple fill the space below with early spring, flapping new leaves to the creek's rhythm. Soon, the trail narrows to a ledge hung above the crowns of alders, then abruptly swings back into the slope. Only half-alert to anything but the nearground, we're jolted by the sight of a glowing tree. Instantly, it leaps out from everything around it.

Radiant, solitary---it seems possessed by a force unknown to any other here, as if the commonness of green had become intolerable, as if all its roots, with precise longing, had broken through a volcanic crust to suck the red, burning flow into every nourished pore. Needle and branch, trunk and clinging moss---all have been lit with something unbelievably foreign. Its very heart feels electrified.

Our feet move. Our eyes fix, unwilling to pull away. Angles of branches change. The trail pushes closer. The glow intensifies and spreads, seeping across our path. We're swallowed into the light. It fills our vision, pours gold over skin and clothes, grips us in the heat of this transfiguration. Then, so slowly, as if to linger on the apology, a dying day calls the light back into itself, to complete its own course. The tree blends back into the forest, giving its body over again to green and earthliness. A last trace of the glow hangs in our eyes and a smile of surrender.

Waves raise their voices. Gwynn Creek is nearing her end, almost home to the waters beyond. Red-orange sun slips deeper into the horizon. Twilight wraps around us as we descend through spruce and pine stunted from their nearly constant struggle with seawinds. The trail cuts into a tunnel of branches matted together against the evening's weakened light. Eyes can gather few clues to guide our feet. Tensed muscles seem to lose their humanness. They become catlike, feeling downward in the second before each planted step, sensing for rock and exposed root and curvature of ground, till the darkness drops away at the end of the tunnel.

Looking back to the dim circle behind us, we follow fog droplets drifting across the opening. They appear more as a hazy illusion than as particles directly in front of our eyes, a strange movement of something almost immaterial, framed in the dark tube of foreground. In simple alertness, we pause to hold the last images of the day. Light patiently drains from the air. Sounds of great waters push through the limbs, fade into stillness and rise again. For a moment, this place seems to reach out, and draw us into the pulse of a larger life.

Reminiscing

At the trailhead south of Tillamook Head, the sun burns away last remnants of morning fog. Rugged hills push against the sea. Our path sparkles with dew, then dips us into a thickness of young forest. Memories of seawind gather in moss, closing around slender trunks, hanging long from stubs of lower limbs. A creek voice threads the air, seeping delicately through the clutter of green forms.

In a leap, we cross the dark waterflow, and the trail bends us toward the sea. Birdsongs now and again drift out of the background. The needled earth allows us to move without a sound, as though we might find a fleeting grace to blend into one day's life here.

What seems like wind rustling on the ridge above begins to take on the mood of the sea. Two voices compete for dominance. Wind asserts from nearby. The surge of waves pushes in from ahead. Sounds merge into one another so fluently we often can't distinguish between them. Our path is leading closer to each, pulling us higher, drawing us seaward in the same movement. Neither power is willing to surrender. Both grow stronger, till we emerge from the forest onto a small point, where the force of water overwhelms the air.

Land drops away completely. A wide view spills into our eyes. Far below, the sea's precise rhythm sweeps in, rushing over sand and stone, cracking at solid walls, gouging farther into an already crooked shore. Across the open water, the line of horizon breaks once at a distant island. Its deserted lighthouse fades and brightens at the touch of thin fog, like a mirage born from some mythical time. To the north, along our course of travel, a strip of beach gathers in long arcs of whitewater spared by surrounding rock. And beyond, defining the limit of sight, Tillamook Head slings its walls up to high carpets of forest, an impossible challenge to a sea that's otherwise able to spread such chaos here.

The mangled landscape around us calls up eons of defeat and victory. A chain of islands lays far into the water, tattered remains of an ancient cape. Two ragged peninsulas of boulders reach up from the sands, trying to remember how they might fit together into walls again. Brown cliffs press their faces out above the waves. From the wall just beside us, a weathered sphinx leans out, locking its gaze on the distance, where green swells align to do battle with stone.

At this height, we're given a shoreline exposed. Stoic forms

poise for the ongoing struggle. A relentless sea charges, welling up from deep strength. Wave upon wave hammers at stone, thundering through the air, exploding with an untamed energy. Two contrary worlds engage and collide.

Somehow, the turmoil below implies an even broader field of engagement. Every face carved in rock, every driven wave, every burst of sound seems to speak a wider message. *If you would come close, you must accept the danger.* A raw freedom whips up from the shore. It curls over us, compressing on skin and bone. It streams through eyes and ears, cutting inward, as if aimed for the very center of being. It demands the battle. *If you choose for closeness, you risk yourself.*

Turning away, we plunge into the shadows. The trail swings inland for a steep descent. A stairway of roots and rocks drops us into the land of old spruce. Except for the giants who decided long ago for a path straight to the sky, the forest speaks a wild randomness. Limbs bend to the fitful wind or twist according to the spruce's own unpredictable nature. Roots scratch out their journeys, through rotting stumps, crumbling logs, anything that smells of available nutrients.

Trunks hook out from the slope. Saplings seize the opportunity, latching onto the old ones with viny grips. Smooth bodies lean precariously over the trail. Their neighbors distort with blisters all along their bark, where clumps of licorice fern settle and prosper. One tree drives into an old snag, feeding from it and at the same time supporting its weight, sinking so deeply into decayed flesh that one life and one death now seem inseparable.

Thick roots hunch their backs to lift the weights of massive trunks higher from their very bases. Even the young spruce drag up the ground below them. Roots become stilts; dark soil becomes a pedestal. The creatures' claws extend, hungry for the flavor and sustenance of this land. Earth flexes back, upward and in, as though she not only endures these demands, but grows stronger, fuller, in the act of mothering.

Spring colors erupt in the foreground. Groves of pink and white starflowers line the trail and gather in unlikely places. They creep up the legs of old spruce and tuck in crevices at the base of their trunks. They spread over rocks and lay out thinly along the tops of melting logs, nudging through settlements of mushroom and deer fern, haircap moss and hemlock seedlings.

Yellow cups of monkeyflower are less inclined to experiment, preferring the simplicity of soil and sun. Cucumber vines drape over the path and send their blossoms up into our faces. Red paintbrush pokes out a show of its tiered petals, embryonic fingers reaching for the light. Leaves of wood sorrel carpet the ground. Sparingly, they sprout flowering stems, as if whole fields of green are needed to create a sprinkling of white beauty. Purple bells of bleedingheart rise above the mat to claim their place in the sun. A few salmonberry blooms hold onto their completeness. Many others give up to the warm days, saving just a petal or two, dying into the green of young berries.

Over a short hump in the forest floor, we quickly sink into marshland. Glossy leaves of skunk cabbage and a jungle of undergrowth close in around us. Earth creases into a series of brief rolls and depressions. The black path snakes through the density, funneling us along what seems like the only course possible. We're cut off from sun, held by a damp, shadowed world so thick even rain and fog must find it hard to penetrate. The dampness begins to feel like the breath of these plants themselves, risen as vapor, congealed against the ceiling of a domed sanctuary, dripped down again to waiting leaves. They inhale, transform, exhale and wait again, a circle of sufficiency, where no outer force might ever find a crack in the shield, where a small space of life, undisturbed, might tend to its own needs. The space allows us, integrates us, accepts our breath as a welcome injection to feed the unfolding of new growth.

Then it heaves us back to the outer world.

Warm light splashes on our hands and faces. A surge of waves reclaims the open air. Scrubby spruce, thimbleberry and salal overtake the hillside, leaving only a narrow channel for our passage. Hints of water and a few small islands filter through the bank of trees below. Slowly, the crashing surf grows bolder. Limbs beside us start to fall away. The trail bends into a steeper slope, cutting a thin terrace across gray rockslides. Our eyes and the air fill with the sea's power.

The descent we'd noticed only in fragments has carried us deeper into her force. She cracks at the bases of island pinnacles, blasting spray high up their walls. Curling again, she whips her green into another white fever, declares her intent with a roar, and slams against the land. Obsessed with the battle, she devours the low rock, digs for the heart of any who stands above her, slashes at the footings of the proudest heights. *If you would come close, you must accept the danger.* She's lured us from the shelter of a high, distant view, to reveal here why even the most rooted stone might tremble at the sound of her approach.

The rockslides die away behind us. Walls of vegetation rise again, screening out the immediacy of the shore. Berry bushes and tall grasses tangle into each other. Stalks of foxglove push to six feet or higher, lining their lavender trumpets along the seaward side. At the next glimpse of open water, a white butterfly stops us in mid-breath, sweeping up into our faces, then flexing casually, playing the breeze with an effortless flutter. It weaves away, side to side, drifts down and sails up, acrobatic, inspired by light. (How can we not fold our hands in silent applause?) No frenzy. No call of necessity. No impulse to feed or mate or otherwise obtain. This is merely a test: what feeling, what unimagined worlds, have come with these new-grown wings?

Tunneling quickly through dense salal, the trail drops us onto a tumble of rock at the back of the beach. We hurry across the boulders, eager to sink our feet in sand. Over a lip of gray stones, the horizon lays out against our eyes, a clean line dividing water from the blue distance. Here, in an openness that feels unlimited, the sea makes peace with the land. Her soft washing disguises all the power we felt earlier. This place will admit none of the furies to the south.

Gone are the explosive cracks that undercut sheer walls. Gone are the rumblings of resistance where land-wedges slice into her strength. No curling swells roar their approach at pinnacles. No spray flies at the wind. No boiling whitewater swallows dark faces. No boulders, once high and proud above the surf, cling together against her to protect the last grains of their dignity.

The fury is drained. She comes as she must---restless, yet quiet, gentle, forgiving. On the sand. On the south point creeping into her with a gradual slope. And there, at the north end of the beach, running sideways along the headland, a tower defiantly shot from the crust of the earth, to say: the water, the greatest of all waters, even she will not pass beyond here.

The hushed voice in the sand fades as we climb above the beach. Our trail hooks in against the headland's flank. From a cover of undergrowth, skeletal forest spreads across the first slope. Widely spaced trees and snags watch over their domain at the edge of land.

Glancing up to the ridge, we're caught by the grace of four buzzards gliding above the spires. Four become five, then six: dark bodies join the pattern as if by magic. Wings lock against the blue. Only the angles of each form decide the course of the flow. Bodies dip and rise, passing closely, realigning, mixing their glides in a circle-dance, spiraling downward, meticulous, unhurried.

Over minutes, they close in on the treetops. The business of hunting has grown irrelevant to the whirling rhythm. Two forms disappear from the circle. The sweep of poised wings continues, between blue above and green below. A body reappears, fitting in precisely, absorbing into the whole motion-without-movement. The slow dance and the deep silence of space behind it remain unbroken.

The spruce tighten again, pulling us into a dim world. A hint of seavoice lingers over the slope. Wind stirs in the high limbs, like the sound of a distant stream. Yet here below, a total stillness hangs around us. Not a leaf or needle responds to the voices. How can they seem not to hear? They know these spoken forces intimately. Even sealed in half-light, sheltered by their own density, these lives can't possibly escape the rhythms on the air. From the tide's daily moods, to steady breezes and wild gusts, to the howling of a winter storm--- the voices must permeate whatever grows in this place. Ferns and starflowers, sorrel and evergreen huckleberry, the shiny heart-leaves of false lily, mosses pouring over rocks and roots and fallen trunks, the old spruce and the hemlock seedlings: all must learn to fuse these voices into otherwise silent lives.

And what human lives have the voices touched? Are these the winds that evoked and carried centuries of native chants? Are these the seasongs that filled the dreams of explorers and pioneers? It's told that this trail approximates the route Captain Clark walked over the headland from his northern camp, nearly two hundred years ago, after a journey that covered half a continent. Looking across into the forest, we follow his movement on a parallel course---there, between those trees, over those limbs, through that cluster of ferns. We imagine into the time and thought of such a distant human presence, watch the buckskinned figure, agile and quiet, laboring over the slope.

This must have felt like the very end of earth, the edge where vast green dropped away at walls hung above the unknowable sea. What curiosity and courage would push an explorer so deep into this raw territory? What difficulties met him on the unbeaten path, in the hoofprints of elk, on the almost invisible routes of native messengers? What uncertainties and possible dangers preyed on his spirit, as he threaded his way through the dense life that would open sight only a moment ahead, and shut out his past only a moment behind? What inkling of an eternal present crept over him as limbs and trunks parted, as limbs and trunks closed again?

Even on the beaten path, we choose our steps with care,

moving quietly, as he might, alert to the meetings of feet and earth. We see the doe at the same time she sees us. Instantly, her eyes betray the panic shot through her heart. She spins away and scrambles back up the trail. Around the next turn, we stop again to look for her. No sound or movement disturbs the forest. Searching over the field of green, we speak out through the trees. She's holding motionless, concealed in a thicket of brush. Soon, she grows wary of the game and the strange presence. With a frantic crash, she gives away her hiding place, charging up the slope to solitude and safety.

The climb begins to draw out sweat. The air collapses into quiet. A light wind, a bird melody dropped from high limbs, the creaks of old trees struggling against their years---the few voices feel superimposed on a wide emptiness. We try to fit into the silence, to become part of this place, creatures caught up in its rhythm. Our eyes switch from the path, to the trees, to the path, to the limbs above. Legs and feet aim for precision. Three quiet steps appear ahead. Three slender trunks pass by. A twig snaps at a second of inattention. The forest quickly renews the air's balance. Three steps unfold. Breath draws in. Three steps push deeper into a soundless world. Our lungs empty. Trunks and branches emerge, grow close, fill our eyes, and slide out of sight.

Fragments of the forest mix into our search for silent landings. Muscle and air and bits of life around us blend into each other. Time slips toward redefinition. Seer and seen, feet and trail, passage and place---all seem to melt together in one movement. Three steps, a breath, a glimpse of fern, a feeling of earth cradled in brown limbs. Three steps, a breath, a massive trunk consuming our vision.

Eyes to the forest. Eyes to the path. Legs bend and stretch. Images flow in steady rhythm, till we turn from a sideward glance and our bodies shock, at the sense of a dark form whipped across the path. Nothing follows but our own muscles working the slope. No sound. Two steps. No lingering clue to another presence. Two steps. A quick probe into the tangle of limbs. No trace, no evidence---as though a bird or shadow had leaped across the trail and vanished. Eyes return to pick out steps, then flash to the side, searching. No sound, no trace. The forest closes back over its mysteries, retreating into still, secretive poses.

Our course levels onto the crest of the headland, weaving us into thin passages among densely packed trunks. As we drop onto the north flank, a cross-trail promises to lead to the sea. Without hesitation, we turn to follow the new path down its slope. Young spruce and hemlock mingle with the alders claiming dominance here. Red-brown stumps of giants wear notches in their sides, testimony to the early days of logging. Out along the forest floor, patches of light spread over chosen swordferns. A family of brownbirds scatters to both sides of the trail, gone too fast for us to see anything but dark bodies and a hint of blue.

With almost every step we plant, black-and-white moths rouse themselves in front of us, lifting up and away into the brush. Curious about their details, we slow our pace and try to see them before they take flight, sneaking in, hunching down, hoping for a close look at the unwary.

They deny us. Our presence hits them with its leading wave a second before we can cut through the camouflage, launching them from the trail just as we close in. Their sense, our eyes---the tension of our near-meeting endures, till one moth allows us to penetrate. Carefully, we ease down. Our faces push close. The wings come into focus, velvet black laid flat against dark soil, a white design scrawled across them, like the torso and legs of a spider from an abstract view. Then---did our breath betray us?---its wings startle like frightened eyes and whip away in a blur. At the next step, and the next, cued to these thumps against the earth, moths ahead spring up and take off in drunken flight, as though our every move ripples the ground enough to snap them from the deepest sleep.

The trail drops steadily through quiet forest. Somehow guarded from the wind, the forms around us seem frozen. Long curtains of moss, arms of alder stretching out bright new leaves, needled branches poked into the maze where trees embrace each other, colonies of tiny blue flowers puffed out like thoughts of winter breath, white blooms of queen's cup hovering against glossy leaves, fans of bracken fern and swordfern sprung through the cover of fallen branches---all seem filled with a fresh clarity. Lacking wind and movement and rustling voice, they amplify from inside, pushing out more intently, calling to the surface a will to live by color and shape alone.

Elk whistles pierce through the stillness, ethereal, disembodied, like the shrill pitch of a coastal buoy haunting night seas. The sounds draw closer and begin to dominate the air. Soon they rise with alarm, insistent and very near, to warn us away from their bed. We slip cautiously through the most threatening tones. The whistles have only begun to fade and calm, when suddenly the forest cracks open. Sky and water surge in, unannounced, as though, by a twist of time, we had ourselves discovered the end of earth, the meeting ground, where powers of forest and stone walls and the incomprehensible sea spill into each other.

A deep carving in the shoreline opens below us. From her swollen energy, the sea unleashes on the land in violent white bursts. Blackrock climbs above the spray, freezing its weathered faces high over the battered lowland. Mosses begin to tint and soften the upper walls. Bare landslides angle up toward the plateau, till clumps of brush are able to dot themselves across the shale. Just before the summit, the speckled brown-and-green cover thickens, anchoring its life to a nearly vertical slope. The rim we stand on bends a crescent from the land, hundreds of feet above thrashing water. Forest presses to the very edge, draping its last roots out to the height, like immense claws yet to sink into their prey.

At the south end of the plateau, the headland's outer reach frames dark cliffs on a background of sky and water. Almost due west, over a quicksilver sea, the island lighthouse drifts in and out of passing fog banks. To the north, from our position, all we can gather is open sea, a brief extension of the forested plateau, and a long drop through empty space.

Running our eyes up and across the walls, sweeping along the lip of the highland, we try to absorb the whole of this place, see the stages of its evolution, feel into the forces that built it. Again and again, we're torn away from the larger view. The sea won't allow us to rest in the beauty of still faces. She captures us with the energy of her whitewater. We pull away briefly, to take in the full scope of what lies before us. She calls us back, like mesmerized children. Not to her vastness. Not to her gray, convoluted rhythm. Not to her dance with flickering light. She demands our eyes at the edge, at the narrow focus where power manifests. She demands us at the heart of the battle.

Something doesn't fit. Our tall perspective has clamped away all sound of the war below. A hush has stolen the air, even as the clashes erupt in our eyes. White furies pound at the fortress walls. Confusions of spray launch for the sky. Splashdowns crush their weight on straining rock. Blow after blow, the sea drives into the headland with a passion that admits no limit. But the furies are muted, dreamlike. None will part the air with a whoosh, or a crack, or the roar that slices boulders from high perches. None will confess the full truth of this wild and turbulent shore.

The world has grown deaf, the sea speechless. Our eyes and ears can't reconcile the flood of images with an air that won't speak them. Can this be the same body that glories in thunder and the fierceness of her own voice? The same that explodes against silence, from swells too full and fast to comprehend? The same that throws driftwood like feathers at a land braced for the impact of her restless power? Long and carefully, we watch her lash the shore. A heavy, unreal quiet is the only reply.

At last, the dream turns us back into the trees. We climb quickly through the young forest and trace upward again toward the headland's summit. As the old spruce gather around us, our strides become less determined. The earth takes our measured steps without a sound. Among the trunks and shadows, we probe once more for intimations of Captain Clark. Trees hide behind one another as we walk, then reappear and hide again, till each finally recedes into the crowd of lives behind us. In the stillness, in the sweep of our eyes, in the images flowing by---we might easily believe not that we're passing through the forest, but that the forest is passing through us.

Feather and Stone

Blanco's winds are feisty today, whipping leaves and needles into a frantic dance. From our campsite, we drop into a spruce tunnel, where the pulse of waves gradually pushes through the rustling nearby. Limbs arch over us with a tight grip, driving the wind upward. The air inside our passageway seems to gel into a heavy substance. Our bodies press against it as though we're not walking earth at all, but wading through some unfamiliar density that seeps around us in slow motion and bonds together again behind us. The closeness of trunks and undergrowth holds our focus to a small world.

At the first glimpse of a mule deer's hindquarters, we pause, then quietly move ahead. She senses us, and bends her long neck to look back, laying her ears forward, keeping her body pointed away for a fast escape. We stop and greet her softly. She pulls her ears back, unsure but not frightened. After a minute of wondering how to act, she casually begins to step away, allowing us to follow at the agreed distance. Glancing from side to side, she scans the undergrowth for a way out. But we're sealed in together, enclosed by solid walls of brush. She stops to look at us with questioning eyes; we stop and talk to her reassuringly. As she continues, we lose sight of her around a turn. Respecting the distance, we hold to the same pace. Not a sound betrays her when she slips from the trail into hiding.

The tunnel opens to a grassy plateau, where the lighthouse and Blanco's outer limit come into view. Almost immediately, the rhythm of our legs touches off a flurry of butterflies. Brown on orange, white on black, colors neatly sectioned on their wings, a distant cousin of monarch or viceroy---some are brave enough to hold their flowers even as we pass closely. But most along the way spring up from their clusters of yarrow, throwing their fates to a wind so strong it seems they can't possibly return. Following the flight and landing of one, our eyes begin to pick out others, till the entire field of white bouquets comes alive with flexing wings. Dozens have flown at our movement. Hundreds more feed in the safety far from the established path.

A vague horizon of sea and sky floats above the highland grasses. As we watch ahead, gray water spreads toward us, growing out of a distant haze. The wide surface of light and motion begins to break into individual swells. With a few more steps, the sweep of coastline unfolds from the plateau's rim. Miles of white beach lay out against the caress of waves, slowly arcing into the contour of a green peninsula. Beyond it, the pyramid of Humbug Mountain surges up from the lowland. And in the remote south, dark slopes lined along the shore hesitantly squeeze their presence out of thick white air.

Far below, a solitary human figure creeps over the sand. A jumble of driftwood stretches away between walls and waves to the north. At the end of the beach, Blanco's form erupts, climbing through boulders and slides to the cliffs underpinning this plateau.

In the long view, we can't make sense of what we see. The cape is always noted and drawn as the westernmost point of this shore. But it feels blunt, dropped away impulsively in a plunge at the wide sea. Land to our south appears to spread much farther into the water. The curving beach, Humbug, even hills inland from the mountain---all, from our point on the rim, seem to exceed the reach of the cape. And the hazy green arms of the coast, at our southern limit of sight, feel as if they could be even miles west of Blanco's walls. Somehow, our eyes ---or the maps---haven't quite seized the truth of this place.

Along the rim, we follow toward the lighthouse. As it draws closer, the cape becomes more and more imposing, soaring up from the beach and tiny islands gathered around, splitting its face into gray ridges and sandstone walls. We'd hoped to cut a path around the base, staying just above the waterline. Through binoculars, we study the route, the angles and footing, the passages that appear most

difficult. Some movements look safe and clean. Others look treacherous, even impossible. The cape feels too powerful, too forbidding, too ripe with visions of a moment's error and helpless bodies slammed against the low rocks.

Instead, we cross east of the lighthouse and leave Blanco to its fitful struggle with the sea. The north flank lays out a much different course, gently dipping a yellow slope down to the sand. In the distance, over two long, curving beaches divided by a river mouth, Blacklock Point juts out from the mainland to define a northern horizon.

Islands scattered along the shore lend a moodiness to the seascape. A few shoot up as dark, jagged cones. Others are slung above the water just enough to hold swells off to their sides, below the rounded tops. And many poke through the surface with profiles so completely worn that they can be islands only from moment to moment. They submerge into each swell, confusing the sea's rhythm into patches of white and translucent green, shedding waterfalls down their hunched backs, emerging black and solid again after the swallowing.

The soft incline carries us onto the beach. Dying waves spread over the sand, pushing their conclusions far along the flat expanse. A cold wind lashes at beachgrass on the foredune. We're forced to work for passage, leaning heavily against the spirit swept out of the north.

Sand stings at our legs, like a needled fog driven down the shore. Textures of the beach mix against our bare feet, from fine sand with only a sprinkling of rocks, to larger grains tumbled through with bits of white shell, to a stretch of pebbled gray, then to a concentration of stones gathered into their own bed.

Our pace falters. Our attention becomes trapped. The stones begin to suck us in. Mind and vision condense into narrow focuses. From our full height, the gathering looks almost uniform. But in close, like a microscope drawing up new layers of sight, our eyes move through a flow of color and form. Peculiarities break out of the gray field: olive and blood-red, amethyst and tan, dark ovals spotted with creamy white, yellow shot through green and red like the rings of surreal planets, rough-cut agates, yet to be worn by sand and clicks against other stones.

We stagger from one focus to the next, absorbed, unaware of any but the small world of the moment. There are gems here such as we've never seen. The unusual catches us, a stone at a time---some shape or pattern, a face or combination of color, that transforms one into something different than all the rest. Gleaming eyes freeze. A hand moves into the field, toward the one among many. It may be a breath of jade-green, an uncommonly deep red or a desert landscape, milky swirls on orange agate, lines of quartz curved into the shape of wings, a white petroglyph impressed on smooth black.

42

No thought or reason guides our movement. Vision and touch and fascination wind into each other. Curiosity shifts from stone to stone. How does it look up close? What's on the other side? How does it change with the angle of light? How does it feel between thumb and finger? We sort through possibilities, turning and examining, saving a chosen few for drying and reinspection. (The sea adds her own sheen to these faces. Wet stones take on the light easily, and only reluctantly give it up to the air. It may not be as simple as we think to appear mute and motionless and void of life.)

The field of color thins and dies out. As the beach returns to sand, we snap back to the larger world. A sense of openness floods through us, and we begin to run along the lip of water. Wind presses hard into our bodies. Loose grains cave together under our weight. Thigh muscles lift up from deep footprints and reach forward to slice through the fast air. Lungs fill quickly, urged by the power of the wind, and push out forcefully to empty back into it. Even held at a half-stride, our movement feels free, fluid, a ripple of humanness spread into the elements around us.

From a dark pinnacle in the surf, a few gulls throw themselves out and begin to cruise the water's edge. They glide by us on a high current, bank around and struggle back upwind, till they pass again. And they repeat the pattern, riding the flow, turning, fighting back against it, each time sneaking glances at us from close range.

Their pretense of hunting doesn't fool us. We've become their spectator sport. Today, we're the novelty, a relief from long days of scavenging and being entertained only by cormorants, who are more inclined to sit on rocks or float passively on the swells than to do anything particularly entertaining. A thought occurs that the gulls might wish they could run. Do they crave a muscular contact with the land, instead of skinny legs and knobby knees and feet that look mostly good for paddling? Could they be as dreamy-eyed for this pulse along the sand as we are for the freedom of flight?

Blanco slips farther behind us. The silhouette of Blacklock slowly begins to take on more distinct features. At the river, we search out a shallow bend and wade, hip-deep, through the clear current. Flocks of birds gather downstream on the river's last bar, separating by kind. Four pelicans plant close to the sea, in sleepy postures, long beaks tucked into their breasts. Gray-and-white gulls rank themselves next, hanging just upstream from broken waves. Brown gulls nestle in against the black-headed terns, as if imagining that something of beauty might be contagious.

A solitary gull splits from the crowd and wings north, holding low along the surf. It sweeps up on the draft and turns to glide, without a movement, down the wind. Just above us, instantaneously, it surrenders to light, to become something almost angelic. Beams reflected from the sea explode on the underside of its wings and torso.

44

The body seems to lose all relation with solid form, seems mutated into a breath of cloud. A glow races over our heads, and so patiently, congeals into feathers again. Feet reach out for sand. Wings fold in. The air empties. The lone figure drops back to the bar and settles in among its clan, indistinguishable from the rest, a master of illusion who simply couldn't decline the chance to practice on a human audience.

Our river crossing has changed the face of the shore. The hill above now spreads a thick forest down its flank. The beach has grayed and built a steep angle up to a driftwood shelf, where logs pile randomly onto one another. Many still wear limbs and roots, conjuring up skeletons of prehistoric sea creatures. Massive stumps thrown on their sides lay roots to the air, like tattered webs that have forgotten how to catch hold of earth. One log anchors an end in the shelf and leans out over the beach, a figurehead, poised and alert, overlooking the restless tumble of waves.

The sea adopts a new strategy against the land. She won't approach gently, but instead condenses her power in a final moment, curling high and fast beside us. All her strength announces in a short, loud thrust at the beach. Momentum dies halfway up the slope, in a blanket of white foam. White suddenly dissolves to gray-green as the foam bursts. For a second, the world freezes in a wave's last breath. Water and sand tense at the line of their meeting. The flattened wave begins to pull away. In the rush of retreat, it snatches at lightbeams and calls them into a sparkle-dance, millions of stars flickering on inverted sky. A gloss lingers over the sand, fading down the slope, slipping between the grains, till all memory of what came before is buried in the crush of the next wave.

And she roars out against the air, this vast life. Behind everything near, behind every green wall smashed into whitewater, through the tracks of a thousand footsteps, she holds to a continuous, overarching voice. We don't know how or why. She might erupt from below, scouring over ridges and valleys of hidden blackrock, the base of these sculptures cut through her surface. Or the roar might come on the trickster wind, compressing sounds from the north---a hundred waves crashing, a hundred broken to their last impulses, a hundred spent and now whispering their retreat, all lifting their solitudes into the wind's race along the shore to speak the collective power in one voice.

Our path weaves unsteadily, following the edge of surf. We dip down as the sea withdraws, to feel the walls of green looming just in front of us. She responds to the boldness, surging high into the slope, forcing us to scurry up along her white lip. Behind us, other waves wash over the crooked line of our tracks. Already, even as our feet scrape through the rough sand, she whittles away at the evidence of our passing.

Blacklock has crept up on us. Its flank serenely rises from boulders strewn around the base, like a knowing laugh at the disarray of eons. Off its crumbled tip, islands jab at the sky, breaking the horizon into pieces that fit among their weathered forms.

From a driftwood heap, we jump to a strip of sand threaded among tall rocks. Light dims as they collect around us. Their shadows sprawl across the sand and dominate the air. With every step, the circle seems to tighten. Voices of waves become hushed. The closeness feels charged, heavy with power or meaning, some hiddenness waiting to emerge. Textures in stone grab at our eyes and draw in our fingers, puzzling. We begin to sense that we've stumbled into a different time, a half-lit corridor where impossibly ancient faces tell creation stories to each other across the emptiness that separates them. Among them, on them, even trying to see with our hands and listen with our eyes, we can gather only bits of the tales.

One boulder pushes out dark pebbles from a crust like smoky sandstone. Another---bleached gray, too smooth to be obviously born from the sand---riddles its body with ruby and emerald stones. One giant digs deep into the beach, just outside the water's range, folding its white skin into ridges and valleys that will deflect all but the most direct westerly wind. Another stretches out to become a slab of rough sculpture. Thick, vertical layers fuse unevenly, dividing into fields tinted red and green and white. Black boulders scatter out among the others, so immense and so round it seems they should have rolled even through the sea, to a home in some lightless canyon far below the swells. Instead they settled here, to strain against warm light and cool nights and their own gravity, till they cracked open, like a rupture of the earth itself or a shearing away of continents. How could so many different faces find this place, this one corner of a wide planet, to bring their unlikeness together?

The giant backs lift us onto Blacklock's slope. As we climb, grasses and lupine give way to crumbled whiterock. The flank wrinkles into small peaks and gulches. We dip and rise, picking our course around slides and cliffs to a last sandstone wall, through a worn groove and up, onto the crest of the point. From here, the height allows our eyes to run over the whole lay of the shore we've traveled. Gray beach and its line of driftwood curl away beneath a forested slope. Two rugged islands poise over a sprinkling of other dark shapes broken through steel-gray water. In the distance, the slice of river starts another crescent of beach that leads back toward the hazy outline of Blanco's form.

We turn and head north along the rim of the plateau, feeling out the open land. Grasses shiver at the moody wind, an impulsive and reckless green field hung above the slow rhythm of waves. A few mini-groves and solitary figures of spruce hunker down in tough postures. A logic of sparseness holds the high ground, trimming away diversity, clipping life back to the hardiest and most resilient.

But as we walk, the more subtle survivors begin to reveal themselves. Irises show first, mixing their tints from light- to deep-purple, all running dark veins like river tributaries down their petals, inward toward yellow hearts. Mounds of lupine billow up, testing every shade of violet, even bleeding into a pale blue. Then others catch our eyes---buttercup and goldstar, vetch and clover, aster and blue-eyed mary---a celebration of color spilled out through the curtain of grass.

The young ones pursue us, like children enthralled by the game---peeking through their cover, hardly able to stifle their laughter, wanting their presence to be known, wide-eyed with surprise at being found---till we come to the end of the plateau. Blacklock falls away to the long sweep of shore. On the western edge below us, a narrow ridge slides its flanks to the waterline. The finger of boulders at its tip cuts the swells in two, wedging through their power, dulling their impact to save this form stood tall and composed against the wide restlessness. In the north, white sands run free, stretching out along cliffs and low-lying forest, till the miles gently coax the land out to another point. And beyond, a misty-green slope pushes even farther into the sea, maybe Cape Arago, but more a distance we can't certainly name.

Wind hurries across the highland, gusting over skin and spruce, whipping at hair and grass, fitting its stream equally around new bodies and familiar lives. Spread as far as we can see, gray water shimmers with light drained from a thickening cloud cover. Waves rise and curl precisely, etching time on the land's many faces. Space feels vast and generous. Almost by reflex, hands come together at the heart, a wordless greeting floated out to the openness.

Slowly, we circle back to our view of Blanco and the day's travel. Clashes of sea and stone fill the air. We're able to pinpoint some sounds: cracks against the walls of near islands, drownings of humpbacks dotted over the edge of the beach, the rush of white streams cascading down black sides, unchallenged waves arcing in till they exhaust themselves.

Yet some of the most prominent collisions appear silent. A thunder from the background consumes them with its untiring presence. Voices of these power points won't distinguish from one another. They gather into one shock of sound, as if the swells build not only raw force but a voice to carry them in, a sound so full of unrestrained energy that it might burst from the gut of Neptune himself, warning stone of the coming furies, intimidating grains wearied of the war, till they surrender at last and tumble helpless through the boiling sand.

Our eyes follow back over the course we've come. An entire day is exposed in one frame. We start to imagine how small we might

50

look at different points along the span. Just below, at the foot of the slope, we might recognize our color and shape. Maybe even there among the boulders, we could judge size by comparing ourselves to white logs and scrubby trees only a glance away. Along the roll of the near beach, pressed between waves and a hill of green, we reduce into dark figures crawling over the lighter sand. And even before the river, we shrink to almost nothing, losing substance with each passing minute as the haze of air wraps over us.

From the place where our forms fade out of sight, eyes continue to trace across the compacted land that only a short time ago stretched wide and full around us. A dim slope gently lays into the river and the sickle of beach beyond it. As the sand curls away, Blanco's walls rise above island-studded water. The clean line dividing earth and sky fractures only once at a tiny ripple we know to be the lighthouse.

The view from there to here drifts into memory. Colors and movements of the present crowd against our vision. Here. There. Now. Then. Places and times and the senses by which we knew them pour into each other. We cross and return from point to point. Legs pumping madly along the beach and up the slopes---no, our muscles and the land slow us. Bird eyes piercing forward as the wings flex--- even the air drags against us. Light compressed to the solidness of a bullet, yes, and shot between two positions. Here and there, now and

then. The world has pulled itself inside out and flipped side over side.

Minds flash back to where we stood this morning, almost in the shadow of the lighthouse. A broad sweep of yellow covered the hillside. Islands lit their walls. The gray expanse pushed in from our left. A strip of green curved out toward the vague profile of a distant point. Heartbeat, breath and footstep---our own immersions in time ---have given us over to the distance.

We've stepped into the looking glass. An imagination at the future horizon has grown to a full-bodied presence, now faintly tied to a speck on lands past. The green has swollen to a full forest, consuming half our field of sight. Islands now hide all texture on these dark, opposite walls. Waves wash in from the right, beaches curl backwards toward the foot of an obscure Blanco. The distance now is where we began, as though we've spun through a vortex of time and place, as though every step minutely changed the face ahead and the face behind, till we can't even recognize the fibers of our own thread.

We've little tangible evidence to prove the fact of our move-ment---a small collection of stones and shells in a coat pocket. No visible form out there surely whips away the veil of doubt. Only a few imprecise details can urge the land or water to answer about the truth of our passage.

We walked the shore. Our fingers rubbed at cold stone. Our ears filled with the rush of waves. Our feet sank deep in the wet sand.

Our eyes---they soaked in the uncountable images that pressed on us from every direction. Step by step, we were certain of the journey.

But the sense of inner time is unraveling. We shoot out and ricochet. Crossing, returning, memory, presence---we're both source and destination of the bullet of light. Body itself begins to feel untenable, a mistake in the choice of a reference point. It seems no less strange to think the land pulled its imagery beneath us in a blur of acceleration. South has been ripped away. North has materialized, as if the spinning planet lurched from its careful design and threw us into an unforeseeable land of reversed images. A space we thought we'd become intimate with has distorted to almost total newness.

Our focus locks on a wave plunging at the beach. It lifts out of the gray mass, builds into a wall of coiled power and spills over, slamming at the sand, churning into a white chaos. Momentum begins to fade in the struggle with the land. The water flattens, reaching, stretching, winning ground, dying to the struggle, dying, just one more foot, one more second. In a final surge, the wave absorbs the dark grains that had been its passion and purpose. Victorious, it turns to carry its prize back to the mother body, and shocks in disbelief at the wall of green only now curling into white.

The race is lived. The end is reached. Exhaustion warps the memory of a beginning into an odd and foreign image. What was real and certain and clear in its time has dissolved in the race.

A hawk emerges from the corner of our vision, perches on a limb at the edge of the forest, looks a minute, and swoops down and away. A few gulls pass overhead. One is curious enough to come in for a close look, dropping twenty feet with a slight change of wing angle, rising again to rejoin the flock. Four yellow finches, wearing black stripes around their eyes, settle with us on the rim of the plateau.

Without warning, fog begins to swallow the picture. Blanco dims and vanishes, like a ghost that never could have held us high over the sea. Then its beach disappears, and the river mouth, the offshore rocks, the long line of driftwood, the slope of gray sand. Gone. Minutes eat away distance and fragile certainties. Only close companions fight for their substance---the water and rocks just below, a faint green from the forest, the finches and a smattering of flowers, the ridge that stretches out toward the tip of this point. Driven through the white air, they linger with us. Doubtless. Certain. All the world we can see.

Of The Wild, Temporary

Who knows how long you've stood here, watching through tall green eyes over this jagged strip of shore? You're the silent one, without apology. Perhaps you spoke once, a long time ago, belching out smoke and impossible chunks of red rock high against the sky. Why else would the ancient ones call you Neahkahnie, the place of fire?

Now, with a road sliced into you, we assume you're thought tame. Do you feel the humans have belittled your sacredness? Do the indifferent ones, speeding by, eat away at your strength and power? Maybe it's crazy to talk at all about your knowing or feeling. (But out of curiosity, did the roar and vibration of dynamite blasting into your western flank arouse any images of past life? And are those otherwise unexplained black boulders down by the creek really a memory of your hot soul?)

From below, you seem clear and simple enough---a bulk of earth and green poised on the background of sky. We expected only a matter of time and sweat to reveal your peak and the broad view of your domain. Why would the human trail labor up your flank if not to push for that conclusion? We kept close track of the way traveled and the course yet to come, to the darkened point above, where blue was seeping all around you. We paused now and again to feel the cool breeze, to feel whether you'd speak from somewhere behind its voice.

Switchbacking through the north, winding along the west, we listened out into your forest. Then you wrapped us around to the south, where one long view opened on town and bay, the roll of hills and the white lines pushing slowly into the shore. As beautiful as it was, it wasn't enough. We couldn't be satisfied with only a hint of your perspective. Your eyes at the summit---they were the goal. We wanted to know, without doubt, why you chose this aloneness, why it seems your sensibility must clarify and quicken in solitude.

On the south face, never seeming any closer to what we believed your peak, the descent began, away, into the valley. We became certain of that steady movement away, and turned, to trace upward again, following back almost to where we'd started on the circle of your flanks. You saw how the beaten path had begun to confuse us, how we checked our bearings against you. Blue left, blue right, the high point between. But we found no sign of any course leading to the blue. The search brought us only two ascents that seemed to meet in a grand view of the coast.

We began to lose faith in the human trail. (You knew it would happen. Still you were mute, even mischievous, refusing to show us to a clear summit, much less tell of past lives. Forgivable silences, if we have any claim at all to ask or be denied or speak forgiveness in the context of you. It's your territory: rule it as you see fit. Long before us. Long after us.)

For a moment, we did think you heard us pleading. We even thought we heard you speak: come up from the west, you said. If the voice was your guidance or our delusion, we still aren't sure.

The beginning of the new approach was easy, slicing through the emptiness between clumps of swordfern, to the cold, windy ridgeline that so distinctly divides out your flanks. The north view, across a deep valley of forest, came through the limbs in fragments. We stayed with the ridge, becoming more convinced of a summit just above. Carefully, we chose our steps on your blue-green stones, threading ourselves around tangled bodies of the many who died to your love of winter storms.

You heard us ask passage over the muscled roots of those who still live here with you, those brave enough to challenge the winds that lash at you from every direction. You watched us climb over and crawl under those brave enough to try, and ultimately fail. We could only give a little to your slope then, dropping around a root system and shattered body that seemed impassable, slipping through the mingled limbs of young ones gathered just below your ridge. Were we truly confronting the untamed side of your character? Or had we simply stumbled into another encounter with our own weakness?

You must have seen how we were struggling for almost every step---awkward, disoriented, taking on silvered moss and the old man's beard, in our hair, on our faces, hung from our arms, as though trying to absorb us into your landscape. Yes, we did wonder if we'd come too far, come too wild and undefined. With you, it's a reasonable question, a simple logic of fear. It stopped us, Kahnie. And then---maybe it was your doing---it left us. We couldn't say why. Your stilling of the wind might have swayed us. Maybe it was our certainty that the human trail could be reclaimed, with a short drop in any of three directions. Something suggested we go on. It was almost as if you were glad for the company, some other intelligence to whom you could reveal subtle features of yourself, even if it couldn't possibly understand or empathize.

The course had become anything but apparent. Your forest gave little clue about direction. We began to question the purpose of our pressing forward. Fighting your gravity and silence, we gave a little more to the south slope, found an elk or deer trail that parallels your ridgeline, settled into the prints of wild creatures, up a little, down a little, weaving over your ribs, erratic, trusting. Maybe we saw the way only because we wanted to believe there was one. Surely the elk and deer know your faces and your soul better than any who merely visit here. When young, they were probably as curious about your upper limit as we are. What's known about you must be passed from mothers as whisperings to the young. Where to find water. Where to find food. Where, when full, to look out on distant lands.

Their paths held us close to the final knowledge. It seemed to be on that ridge, where we sensed blue as much by the smell and sound of the cold wind as by anything we saw through the limbs. And you watched us break beyond even this indistinct course, pushing through the damp life and lifelessness you allow on your flanks. Yes, by then, even knowing the need for humility, we were pushing---our passion for an answer against your passion for silence. We were aiming for the blue. If you'd deny us that, we'd ask for a wholehearted denial. And our instinct did lead us back up to that line, where you hold north and south together.

You could see then we were close. You knew we studied your profile carefully, trying to feel out the physical placement of things. A rise of stone and earth. A dip to the trunk that still toils against these winds from wherever. Down here. Up here. Our eyes settled on this hump in your spine, this mound, this one particular stone that's highest above all nearby.

Is it here, Kahnie, on this point where we feel the dropping east and west, where we know the dropping north and south? Is it here, on this green stone that may never before have felt the human weight? If we step onto that stone and call it the summit of you, Fire Mountain, will you scoff at us? Will you burst from your core with rage and ridicule? And long after you've buried us deep in the glow of your anger, will you then speak openly to other wanderers, about the day of fools who dared to think they'd met your summit?

If you won't answer or show us otherwise, we can only say, by our eyes and judgment, it's here. You smile at the brashness? Forgive us our youth. Do you remember your own, when you volunteered your being to the hot belly of the earth and exploded from the ocean floor? Do you recall your words, when you told her, like the tactless child you were, of your dreams to reach not only above the wide sea but high into the clouds? That you stand here as you are, towering over this world---the simple fact betrays your own faith and your own youthful will to danger. Even if you've grown intolerant with age, that memory must linger in the soil and stones here, among the lives draped over your flanks.

If you won't speak, how are we to know? Belief is our only alternative.

Of course, we'll not say we had any secret knowledge of you. We'll admit only that your silence forced us to trust our senses, and believe we met you on the summit. Brash maybe, not disrespectful. We *hope* you hold many secrets close. We might only think less of you if you showed all. Do you see our dilemma---wanting to know your life intimately, afraid that the final knowledge would be the end of mystery and dreams? You're wise to leave us with doubt about this particular green stone. We'll believe it's compassion, not scorn, that holds you silent.

We can easily accept that there's no grand view from here, no broad spectacle to reward the effort that led to this conclusion. The branches between us and the blue, these lives who endure, the remains of those who tried and succeeded for their times---don't you know? They mean far more to us than a brief glimpse of rugged coastline, far more than simply another angle on what we'll see again, next time the highway carries us back this way.

If this hard-won place is merely a false summit, Kahnie, if confusion and compromise have misled us about destination, the struggle was more for itself than for the goal. If we've missed your peak, we've come close to you. The twigs and needles tangled in our hair, the moss hung from our clothes, the black soil drying on our fingers, the stains from wet bark rubbed against our skin---if these are marks of the unhuman, we're so many determined steps closer to your wild heart.

Leaves On A Stream

North of Drift Creek, the old forest presses an edge down against the road. A stripe of trail immediately tucks us in among the trees. Just as trunks close together behind us, we reach the sign marking the wilderness boundary. Our path cuts a slow arc up to the ridgeline, peaking in the glow of afternoon light. A gentle descent begins.

We've come in the calm after a storm. Fresh-fallen branches are scattered over the trail---white-barked fir and hemlock, red-barked cedar, all still wearing vibrant green. The canopy has been swept, shedding mostly small growth but even some large limbs that must have held out through many prior lashings. One sharp turn in the path adds a more ominous tone to the force that preceded us. A large fir, apparently undiseased, has torn loose and laid its body across our way. Around it, the forest floor seems to have surrendered to chaos. From the evidence, we can only believe brother wind came in with a fury.

Cones of hemlock sprinkle out through the downed limbs, promises of new life strewn among images of destruction. Our eyes begin to divide out the trees, trunk by trunk. The few cedars won't be mistaken, running fibers up in delicate lines, peeling away thin bark in orange threads. If they deviate at all, it's only to create waves at their bases, like wind-ripples on a lake. Fir and hemlock demand a keener sense. Saplings often disguise their identities, forcing us up to verify by the needles. But the older firs take on a brown tint and cut deep valleys in their bark, breaking their lines out of a clear vertical pattern. Hemlocks hold to gray, running shallow grooves up in nearly continuous lines. Without much higher investigation, even by the sea of promises spread at our feet, we can feel how the hemlocks have grown to dominate the forest.

Along the way, red snags hang precariously above us. One trickles bits of itself onto the trail. Another gives way to an avalanche, pouring sweet-smelling chunks two feet deep across our path. We hurry through each danger zone, wincing at the thought of bad timing. Benevolent as it is, the forest offers no absolute guarantees. Tired skeletons will crumble. Tall trees will heave their roots and thunder against the earth. High branches will sneak from the sky to crash without warning. Possibilities will meet their time, regardless of the small creatures who might hope for safe passage.

Snags and deadfall fit with the feel of this place. Faces of death and decay spill across the stage---fresh-falls, logs just beginning to sprout moss in patches along their bark, red-rot flaking off in the layers that were once rings of living cells, lumps of what used to be wood now all but integrated back into soil. The forest is following through its natural cycle. It was left untouched, for whatever reason ---too remote, too steep to log easily, maybe an oversight from days when the land seemed infinite and the harvest inexhaustible.

Now, this plot of wilderness receives official protection to stay on its own course. Small lives feed from bodies that have passed into afterlife. Saplings build their strength under limbs of their ancestors. And the old ones grow into their majesty, till age overcomes them or the elements bring them down. Whatever enacts the final moment, even if it seems to us premature, no death here can be called unnatural. The primal forces rule this land and decide its flow---what endures and how it grows, what dies when, and how these individual lives meet their ends.

As the course pulls us deeper, we feel the impossibility of knowing all the faces here. Our fingers run over the skin of an immense old trunk. Above, a dark woodpecker scratches its grip upward, testing with light taps, scraping higher, testing again, till it hears a likely site for an insect colony and agitates its knock at the promising bark. A brownbird flits beside us, tiny as a hummingbird, chirping when we speak, then disappearing into the safe tangle of brush. A hemlock to our right considered becoming two, splitting into nearly complete twin trunks, mending itself back into one solid form as it gained height. To the left, through the first rank of trees huddled against the trail, ten or more saplings have settled together in a clean line, sucking at the fluid and flesh of a rotting log.

Yet so much slips by unnoticed. Seeing near, we ignore the distance. Focusing long, we can't gather in the lives passing right beside us. The field is too broad, our eyes too slow and concentrated. The act of seeing becomes a choice for one among many impressions available in the moment. Attention and desire aren't enough to admit the whole of this place. We resign just to absorb what comes---near or far, left or right, above or around. Our eyes will capture only fragments. An undreamed wealth of other images will slide around the edges of our perception.

Hemlocks lead us into the homeland of old firs. These wrinkled giants always feel like the guardians of silence, like wisdom itself looking down over all below and somehow guiding the many forms holding close to earth. But soon we begin to see the tortures inflicted here, the sadnesses endured by those who would carry and spread the wisdom. Many of the old ones have snapped. Jagged stumps remind survivors of emptiness felt in the loss of comrades. Splintered bodies

lay out along the course of this wind tunnel. Others have broken deep in the soil and ripped themselves out whole. Root masses flail at the air, speaking the wisdom even in death, as they give home and hope to seedlings, vine maple, swordferns, any life inclined to feed from the draining of a great energy.

The trail dips into the crater left by one fallen giant. Its fully exposed root system rises beside us. Selective roots have been hacked off to clear the path. Cuts reveal growth rings much like those of a tree itself, but stretched to one side, as though redirection may have been necessary to reach a pocket of nutrients.

In the closeness of the crater, standing in soil that not long ago fed the giant through these sprung roots, we imagine back into the life of this one being---how it defended itself against the onslaughts here, bent its supple body year after year, sent its roots deeper and wider to add stability and feed the new green pushing outward. But in a final hour, the majesty crumbled. Perhaps there was even fear. The slope, the wear of years, the force building in this tunnel, became too much. Wind determined to prove its rule, pressing at the limit of the tall one's strength, surging into a fatal gust while the giant was bent and vulnerable. The obsessed presence on the air might have cut loose a victorious laugh, a final, frightening breath, as it heard the deep crack, felt shivers of death in soil and fiber, saw the earth heave in a wide circle, knew the old one had leaned too far this time to recover. And the massive body surrendered, with a long sigh of giving up life, brushing its limbs against neighbors who watched, helpless and horrified, thundering down to crush whatever lay east.

Slowly, we rise out of the giant's footprint and continue, unsure if the lingering sense of distraction is wonder at the power of life, or wonder at the power of death. Across a small runoff, we see that the old ones haven't been the only casualties. Signs of the recent fury impose all around us. Over the course of fifty feet, a dozen or more middle-aged trees have dropped across the trail. We slide over a few, and seeing more ahead, sidetrack higher. Leaning into the angle of a new-fallen hemlock, we scramble up to the gnarled roots now futile against the air. The slivered stumps and uprootings are all confined in a small diameter. Healthy trees circle around the destruction, as if a tornado touched down with precise intent, or an impetuous wind, for one devastating second, gave in to possession by a demon not of this earth, shearing life from a few and merely howling through the limbs of survivors.

The breeze drifting over us now seems out of context against the shattered imagery. Unheard, subtle across our skin, filled with a freshness of sea-breath---today the wind feels content to fan the vine maple and curtains of moss hung from the branches around us. An almost mournful peace has reclaimed the forest, broken only by our footfalls and the sound of owl dreams floated down from the canopy.

69

As we cross out of the wind tunnel, our descent becomes more pronounced. Trunks grow leaner and tighten in against one another, adapting to the ways of steep soil. Light weakens under the mat of limbs. The path tapers to a ledge cut from the hillside. The quiet becomes almost tangible, another presence settled into the forest. Every glance meets only fixed poses. Motion seems unknown here, as though time itself might have forgotten this place. Even the rhythm of our legs begins to feel unlikely, till two white-faced nuthatches stop in, twitching their heads at the sound of our voices, curious about these odd phenomena, these steady thumps in the stillness of their day, these blue bodies cutting through newly-strung spider threads.

The slope drops off sharply. The trail whips us through a series of switchbacks, insisting on a quick pace through our final passage to the creek. Almost instantly, her song overtakes the air, as if she's decided this exact moment to part from the silence now grown familiar. Long steps in the forest collapse into a dim past. We're being thrust into a newness we've only begun to sense. A liquid glow slips between the leaves. The shadowed world of bark and limb begins to dissipate. With only a few more steps, the current floods into our eyes.

The meaning of crystal-clear leaps out at us. She seems to shine from within, beaming her own rays out at the open sky. Wide, exuberant, like joy itself given a physical body---she commands the air, lifting the full voice of a rapids. Still unbelieving, we climb to a vantage point, up a huge boulder sunk in the bank. Her many moods crowd together into one perspective.

Upstream, she plays out a gentle face, dropping shallow over stones lined across her bed, stepping through her shelves with calm persistence. Directly out from us, she narrows, racing around boulders, splitting into three points of passage. A sweep of dark water carves its pool from the opposite bank. The flow on center churns and whitens in a fall that demands most of the creek for itself. The channel just below gives up volume for a bold voice, overpowering the sound of all other movements we see.

Beside our boulder, a jam of logs and branches allows water to seep through sparingly, forcing the creek to swell and bend around with the rest of her movement. She broadens again and washes over an alder fallen from the near bank, still holding this year's leaves on its upturned branches, fighting off the drowning in whatever roots continue to work the soil.

Downstream, she gradually stretches her banks, settling into an almost lazy rhythm, floating through the approach to another shelf. The next fall can only be presumed. Our angle allows us to see the peak where dropping begins, but not the fall itself or the aftermath. A single point of light sits atop the shelf, flashing like a star where dark water aligns for the drop.

Along her course, other lives mingle into the picture. Dragon-

71

flies dart across the surface, cutting an erratic path from bank to bank. A lone swallowtail dives and rises on the breeze pushing against the waterflow. Moss-heavy limbs of alder and maple arch out over the creek. One sapling, driven by an unseen energy, shakes last leaves on skinny branches, while all the trees around it hang to their stillness. High above the water, stacked downward branch by branch, strands of spiderwork gleam with stories of daring leaps into the wind. And from the far shore, a whole forest of old-growth sprawls over the slope, hovering above pools and falls, bends and rapids, like a deeply calm force attracted to this life that sings a love of restlessness.

Our eyes are drawn into the realignment just below, the swirl of the creek's dark and white and sparkling faces. Her power condenses in a surge through the narrows. Boulders disrupt the freedom, dictating where she'll funnel and churn, or, by their absence, where she might flatten and make peace with herself. All that lies before us slips into a dance of movement and fixity. Forms locked in their postures dangle against a speeding current. Rhythms of water define and flex and change at every glance. Each focal point, each distinct impression, seems filled with the two forces, as though a veil has been lifted on the balance, as though our sight and our very being could simultaneously penetrate both absolute stillness and perpetual motion.

This stream, this life they call Drift Creek---how could she be

imagined one thing? She shapes and maneuvers entire worlds inside herself. Swelling upward just before a large rock, she bubbles at the play of contrary elements: water and stone give birth to air. Droplets reach high from the rapids and evaporate against the background. Larger drops spit up, claiming individual form, plummeting back into the gravity of the larger body. From the depth after a fall, she accelerates again, gushing up at the next obstacle, spilling over it, a thin curtain rippling with the force of her descent. Then she hides, apparently motionless, but driving under the surface for a silent emergence, like a spring pushing up from her bed. She runs sideways into a dark valley between peaks of liquid light, and in the next movement, curls against herself. The downflow reverses, to lean upstream in a surf caught by the breeze, an immense crystal changing form in every instant and so changing how it patterns the light within.

Always---this changing of light, an incredibly fast flow of beams becoming darkness and exploding again, as if light itself is plunging forward, as if this living freedom, within the limits of her power, internalizes the light, absorbs and yet proves the otherness, sweeps the other down an irresistible course. Water becomes light, and light becomes water,---these are the raw elements from which she creates her transient worlds---till alder and stone, the paths of sun and stream, resolve into a dark, quiet running, another tone of voice, another mode of appearing.

Sitting above her, watching, listening, feeling the movement of our breath, we become another element, an aspect of the surrounding scene. Yet we can't give ourselves completely. The passion of the creek, the strength of stone---both energies feel so confident, so clear about their natures, so certain of purpose. We suspend in their collisions like something else, a middle way, a curious third force of being that changes and yet stays the same, grounds in the moment but inevitably moves forward. We try to feel that unity of purpose. It eludes us. How could the human life be so one-pointed, so fluid and restless, or so fixed and unwavering?

We look to the trees for kinship, as though our hearts and minds need some form here to cling to, some part of this story to hold as our own model for a wild core fitted to a wild world. Attached to earth, pulsing and redefining from within, swaying to the wind that drifts over our surfaces---we and the trees know the wind. We know the softness and the power, the feeling on bark and skin, through needles and hair. Its pressures work on us equally, this force that can only be felt, never seen except in a touch on other forms. The water lives out its course. The stone lives out its determined posture. We and the trees must throw our fates to a wider current, moods that might rush in and catch us unaware, an unpredictable spirit that feeds our lives and yet ultimately, in a moment of fury or a last peaceful breath, will sweep them away.

This world around us seems full, spilling over with almost visible feeling---the creek's lighthearted dance, the patience of stone, the determined pulse of trees, the smooth and measured wingbeats of a butterfly, the simplicity of crawdads and tiny creek snails rummaging for food in slack waters.

We're all of these, and we belong, momentarily. These unfamiliar hearts have slipped in for a day, covered by the silence of mosses and old trees, to meet briefly with the lives that inhabit this valley. And they'll leave again, nomads wandering from home to home. We're native here, the same as every other life settled into particular form. Yet so very often, against our will, we feel like spectators, watching across an unbridgeable gap.

The sun is dipping quickly, easing bright light to gold. The turning world calls us back from our quiet post, on a boulder beside crystal water in an ancient forest, where reverence is natural and immersion sometimes possible. Feet dig upward on the trail that leads both in and out. We seal away again as capsules of being, bordered by the tips of our fingers, the drums of our ears, the lenses of our eyes, a surface of skin pushing back at the breeze. Something of these characters goes with us. Something of us will stay behind, if only a warmth on the air that's filtered through our lungs. And it's not clear if these solitudes, these physical identities, have grown more real or more imaginary for having traded breaths with this place.

Afterword

We've been blessed with time to explore the life of some beautiful places. Our motivations were mixed, and they flowed into each other. Call the reason for these journeys a love of beauty and simple fascination with the process of the natural world. Call it love for the sea's thunder and love for the silence of old forests. Sometimes it was a need for the inner peace that seems to come easily on the trail. At other times, it was an urge to remember how human being fits into the bigger picture, this drama of a planet running its course through black space. Maybe our feet were even aimed at some holy grail---a fragment of enlightened understanding, a few moments of knowing sacredness, not as a concept, but as a truth flowing clear and vital at the fringes of our limited senses.

These places renew our feeling for the deep current. Forest and stream, beach and headland---all feel connected to a primitive freedom at the core of our own lives. We might call it Great Spirit, this intelligence that powers heart and brain, the rhythm of days and seasons, the movement of rivers and seas, the inner workings of every cell and creature possessed of life. We turn to the wild not only to witness the beauty, but to feel the magnitude, and maybe an accident of clarity that rings through us like a cosmic wake-up call.

Poetry surrounds us here. A moth's aimless flight. The glide of a raven or gull. Old spruce dripping off morning dew. Light trapped in droplets on a spider's web or a flower's petals. A dance of limbs and leaves in autumn winds. Rain drifting weightless against a green background. Whitewater exploding into rainbow spray on stone faces.

The poetry is here. We try just to breathe it in, and fit our lives into it. Later, we'll hope for words to approximate the living reality, knowing it to be much like the fog that haunts the coastal valleys. We can see it, step into it, breathe it, let it penetrate our pores. But even with the best intention, we can't close our fingers around it.

The journeys we've spoken confirmed our belief that the wild worlds do love a gentle and respectful human presence. The ways each of us feels that love will be as different as our personal perceptions of beauty.

Go walk the forest and the shore. Stay alert. Keep your eyes and ears ready. Keep your mind in the moment. Keep your heart open and vulnerable.

Our words will become a distant memory, when you push your face to the wind, push your feet through their unique landings on a turning earth, push your being into a day that will never be repeated. With a change of weather, a change of season or light or mind, each wild place becomes new. And each meeting with it is a first time.

Additional copies of **The Meeting Ground** are available directly from the publisher. For each copy ordered, send $9.95 plus $1.00 postage to:

Windshadow Press

Box 207-A

Westlake, OR 97493

Future volumes planned for the *Journeys Into Wild Places* collection include explorations in central Oregon, the north Cascades, the Olympic Peninsula and southeast Alaska. To receive notice of these volumes as they're released, ask to be placed on our mailing list.

Windshadow Press

"Dedicated to the spirit of the wild country"

Member of the Northwest Association of Book Publishers
Member of COSMEP---The International Association of
Independent Publishers